SEEDS OF FAITH

Hope

SEEDS OF FAITH

Hope

Words of Faith from
NORMAN VINCENT PEALE

Ideals Publications · Nashville, Tennessee

ISBN 0-8249-4641-3

Published by Ideals Publications, a division of Guideposts
535 Metroplex Drive, Suite 250, Nashville, Tennessee 37211
www.idealsbooks.com

Editor, Peggy Schaefer
Designer, Marisa Calvin
Cover photograph: Steve Hamblin/Alamy Images

Printed and bound in Mexico by RR Donnelley
10 9 8 7 6 5 4 3 2 1

ACKNOWLEDGMENTS
All scripture quotations, unless otherwise noted, are taken from The
King James Version of the Bible.

When you live with hope in your heart, in your mind, and in your spirit, you have discovered one of life's most powerful secrets of success.

—NORMAN VINCENT PEALE

FOREWORD

Throughout his long career, my father, Norman Vincent Peale, valued no message more than that of the importance of faith in each of our lives. In fact, before the title was finalized, *The Power of Positive Thinking* was called *The Power of Faith*. It was that important to him.

Growing up in the Midwest at the beginning of the twentieth century, Dad learned about faith at his parents' knees and in the pews of small-town churches. Faith in God, country, and fellow man, and the saving message of Jesus Christ filled his youthful days. He learned oratorical skills by listening to the great preachers of the day,

who went from town to town, bringing countless people to faith. He became filled with faith messages, and they never left him.

When the personal call came for him to enter the ministry, Dad was well equipped with deep faith, a gift for communicating, and a love of people. His writings were full of anecdotes of the faith journeys of countless people he met along the way. By their examples, he was able to lead others to a life of faith. His was a great calling, and I think we can all agree that he succeeded.

As you read, I hope you enjoy the messages in this book and that it brings deeper faith into your life.

—*Elizabeth Peale Allen*

Be of
good courage,
and he shall
strengthen
your heart,
all ye that hope
in the Lord.

—Psalm 31:24

*H*ope springs eternal in the human heart. And it is well that it does, for we cannot live without hope. But with it, we *can* live successfully. It makes no difference how much difficulty people experience; with hope, they can still go forward.

Hope! What a wonderful word it is! Write it

indelibly on your mind. H-O-P-E. It is a bright word—shining and scintillating and dynamic, forward-looking, full of courage and optimism. With this word, let us begin each day.

What lies beyond the threshold of today, you do not know, nor do I. We can speculate, but we do not know. Inescapably, however, we must cross that threshold. And with the golden gift of hope, we can cross confidently, eagerly, optimistically.

This life is not easy! It is often fraught with pain and suffering. But hope gives you a lilting upthrust that takes you above the suffering.

The Bible contains truth that cannot be changed

or invalidated, and verse eleven of the Forty-second Psalm states, ". . . hope thou in God: for I shall yet praise him, who is the health of my countenance, and my God." What power is in this text!

Do you truly realize the power of words? Words spoken by an orator can electrify multitudes of people. Words are alive. They can destroy; they can create. Words can break down and words can build up. The kind of words you keep in your mind ultimately determines who you are, what you become.

Hope can release the potential within us. The fact is—and we don't hear it said often enough—

that every one of us has more potential than we think we have.

Don't ever say to yourself, "This is it. This is what I am. I have to settle for what I am." Reach for your potential. If you expect potential, if you hope potential, then you will manifest potential. There isn't anybody who, by application of this great word, *hope*, can't live a bigger and more creative life.

Once, while visiting Switzerland, I had dinner

with friends at an inn that was some four hundred years old. And on the dining-room wall in this inn, I saw this inscription in German, which I copied down:

> *Wenn du denkst es geht nicht mehr,*
> *Kommt von irgendwo ein lichtlein her.*

In English this reads:

> *When you think everything is hopeless,*
> *A little ray of light comes from somewhere.*

Isn't that lovely? And this sentiment is nearly four hundred years old.

Where is this "somewhere"? It is inside your own mind. On the surface your mind may become dark and hopeless; but Almighty God

And thou
shalt be secure,
because there
is hope....

JOB 11:18

has established Himself in you, deep within you, and nothing is hopeless. You are a child of God, and hope has been planted in you by God.

When things are getting you down, remember that little ray of hope—that light that comes from somewhere. That light that comes from God, of whom it has been said, "With men this is impossible; but with God all things are possible" (Matthew 19:26).

Cultivate the conviction that you are not alone, that God is with you. Remember that Jesus said, "I am with you always" (Matthew 28:20). If darkness has settled deeply in your mind, just open it up and let in this little ray of light.

You may think, "Why, sure, I know that God is with me." But do you really? You must build your life on that certainty. If your wife or husband is sitting alongside you, you know it, don't you? You have no doubt about it. It means something to you.

Well, God is even nearer than that. "Closer is He than breathing, and nearer than hands and feet," Lord Tennyson wrote. That means He is part of you. When you really believe this and really practice it, then no matter what life brings you, it will not get you down.

I gave a talk in Albany to a group of people celebrating the 325th anniversary of the First

Reformed Church of Albany. The sturdy Dutch Christians who came into the New World in the seventeenth century believed in freedom, in God, in the love of Jesus Christ, and in the dignity of the individual under God.

At this gathering, I met an upstate New York politician, a man who had been around the state house a long time. He was a lawyer by profession. I liked him, for he impressed me as a straight shooter.

He said, "I went to New York City some years ago to hear you preach. I had read some of your writings, and I thought I'd go down and hear you preach. You put it together pretty well. But," he added, "you didn't get across to me. Your ideas seemed theoretical."

"Did you ever come back?" I asked.

"Yes," he said, "I've been back lots of times. I was there three weeks ago."

"Why did you come back?"

"I usually stayed at a nearby hotel," he replied, "and there wasn't any other place to go. I was there one Sunday when you said one of the most stupid things I've ever heard from a preacher."

"What was that?" I inquired.

"You told about a fellow who was having a hard time," he recalled. "He was almost defeated

Optimism is the faith that leads to achievement.

Nothing can be done without hope or confidence.

HELEN KELLER

and he came to you. You told him God could pull him through if he would get close to God. Well, so far I was with you.

"But then you told this man to go home and when he got into bed to pull a chair alongside the bed and imagine that Jesus Christ was sitting in it. He was to talk to Jesus and tell Him that he wasn't afraid anymore because he knew Jesus was going to sit there and watch over him all night long. Now just think how many people Jesus Christ would have to sit with! There was no sense to it.

"Then you told the man that when he went to

lunch, he was to pull a chair up to the table where he was sitting—no matter how many people were with him. If anybody asked, 'What's that vacant chair for?' he was to say it wasn't any of their business. But in his own mind, he was to see Jesus in that chair. You said that you gave this advice to him to make him know by this simple device that God was with him.

"Well," my new acquaintance continued, "I came back to Albany saying to myself, 'That's the silliest thing I have ever listened to.' But my difficulties continued to defeat me. So one night I pulled a chair up beside my bed. I didn't even tell my wife what I was doing. But I put my hand out on that chair. Nothing happened the first night, nor the second. But I kept on doing it until one night I felt an answering handclasp."

I could see tears in his eyes as he continued, "Even today I don't go to sleep at night without first talking to Him. I don't pull the chair up anymore. I know that is only a device. But I have found that God actually is with a person who will be with Him. And since then, nothing has ever been able to get me down."

"A little ray of light comes from somewhere" . . . from that comforting Voice that said, "I am with you always." Feel that assurance; feel the sense of His presence and hang on to it.

One summer my wife and I were in England. And on a typical English summer day—cold, dark, and rainy—we went down to Chartwell, where Winston Churchill lived for many years and especially during the war. What a beautiful place it was, overlooking the rolling lands of Kent, which had the greenest grass you ever saw.

Outside the house we were shown where

Churchill used to stand every evening during the dark days of the Battle of Britain—wearing an old hat on his head, chomping on the inevitable cigar, and watching the German bombers coming over in great waves. From Chartwell he could hear the reverberations of explosions in the center of London. He could see the flames. In a field nearby they still have one of the little Spitfires, the fighter planes with which the RAF fought off the Germans.

The woman who served as our guide was an old friend of the Churchills. I asked her, "Did Winston Churchill ever lose hope?"

She laughed, "Churchill? No. Hope was built into him. He never expected anything but ultimate victory." That is why some men become immortal. They stand against every defeat, because they have hope built into them.

Well, you may think, "I'm not Churchill; I'm just a regular human being. I get assaulted by the difficulties of life. Things that I plan go wrong. Things that I want don't come to pass. I am struck by trouble of one kind or another: illness, pain, weakness, prejudice, mistreatment."

Certainly you are! But don't allow these things to defeat you. Not when you have God in

Hope thou in God:
for I shall yet praise
him for the help of
his countenance.

PSALM 42:5B

whom you can hope, who will help you yet to praise Him, and who will put such a glow of victory and health in your countenance that life will be a thrill.

If you never stop fighting, you will never be defeated. Build up hope and expectation in your mind and in your heart. Use the text from the great Book. You have heard these verses before, no doubt. Now write them on your consciousness. ". . . hope thou in God: for I shall yet praise him, who is the health of my countenance, and my God." And from Psalm 62:5, "My soul, wait thou only upon God; for my expectation is from him."

If you expect little things from God, you will get little things. If you expect nothing from God, you will get nothing. But if you expect great things from God, He will draw out of you your self-revealing potential. You have it. You can release it. So take the words and walk with them and live with them and think with them and pray with them. Grab onto the power of hope.

*S*torms sweep down upon human beings individually. And they sweep down over society. But if you hope in God and do the right thing, storms pass after a while.

No one ought to go through life without developing a philosophy about storms. Storms toughen wood; storms plow up earth; storms test human beings; storms are hard. But one great thing about storms is that they always pass. And the things that are deeply rooted in the truth of Almighty God endure. So if you are in harmony with God, you can have hope no matter how furious the storm.

While visiting the town where I grew up, I saw an old tree that must have been a hundred, maybe even a hundred and twenty-five years old. And I remembered a night, years ago, when my brother Bob and I were small boys.

My grandmother had just put us to bed when a terrible storm came up. We could hear the wind whirling around the house, making a deep, whistling sound as though it came out of a vortex. And then came the flash of lightning, followed by a clap of thunder. The rain was hurled in great sheets against the windows; the house shook. Bob and I were scared, and from where I lay, I could see, silhouetted against the window, that great tree. Seeing how violently it was being

*Hope elevates,
and joy brightens
his crest.*
JOHN MILTON

tossed by the storm, I was suddenly filled with terror. I always have loved trees, and I loved that one. I turned to Bob and cried, "That tree will never outlast this. It will go down."

We jumped out of bed and scurried downstairs to where my grandmother was sitting by a kerosene lamp. A dyed-in-the-wool Methodist, she was reading the *Christian Advocate*. We cried out, "Grandma! Grandma!"

"What's the matter?" she asked calmly.

"The tree! It's going to go down."

Well, my grandmother was a wise Christian woman. She bundled us up and took us out on the porch in the wind and rain. She said, "Isn't it great to feel the rain on your face? Isn't it great to get out here in the wind? God is in the rain. God is in the wind. Just look at that tree. That tree is having a good time with the storm. It yields to it, bending one way or the other. It doesn't fight it. It cooperates with it. It is playing with the storm. It is laughing with the wind and the rain. I don't think it will go down. It will be there for a long time to come. Now, you go to bed, boys. God is in the storm, and all storms ultimately pass."

So we went back to bed. That was many, many

years ago. Storms come and go, but a great tree stands. It stands because it has driven its roots deep down into the earth. That is why it can grow high. That is how it rides out the storms.

When people crash under storms, when they go to pieces in some way, they do not have the proper root system. Send down into the soil of your life the three great roots of faith, hope, and love, and nothing in this world can shake you, for you will be living in cooperation with Almighty God.

So pull yourself up—physically, mentally, spiritually. Do it by filling your mind with the Bible and with hope. "Hope thou in God: for I

shall yet praise him, who is the health of my countenance . . ." (Psalm 42:5). As you hope in Him,
trust in Him, and serve Him, you will have health
in your countenance because you will have health
all through you—body, mind, and spirit.

A good many years ago, Mrs. Peale and I pur-
chased a farm in Dutchess County, New York.
One early spring day, while walking around a bit,
I saw nature at work. The snowdrifts had only
just left Dutchess County. But even before they

were completely gone, the tulips were coming up, as if they didn't understand that they shouldn't push themselves up in the midst of snow. That day they just covered the place. They hadn't blossomed yet, but they were up. And there were crocuses around the edges of tree trunks, coming up out of the dry grass. And the hillsides had a kind of dark pink all over them, with multitudes of buds ready to come forth.

On this farm we have an old apple tree. The tree man tells me it is over ninety years old. He, naturally, would like to cut it down, saying there is nothing more we can do for it. Of course, I respect his opinion, but if you take care of a tree, prune it and feed it and love it, it will do well. So I have never let him take this apple tree down, and the tree man thinks I'm very foolish.

At one time I am sure this tree had a diameter of about two feet, maybe even three feet. It was a big old apple tree, and it must have had a wide spread. Now there is only about a tenth of the trunk left—just a shell on one side and a few branches reaching out from that. But I like this old tree. And that spring, after living ninety years and with practically all of it gone, what was the tree doing? Shouting that it was finished? Not on your

Now the God of hope fill you
with all joy and peace in believing,
that ye may abound in hope . . .
ROMANS 15:13

life! It was putting out buds. I stood there and talked to it and said, "You foolish old tree, don't you know you should be dead?"

And it was as though it looked at me and answered, "Who says I should be dead? Why, my good friend, don't you know it's springtime and there is an impulse of life, a surging power, within me and I'm trying to live out my destiny?" That tree is a positive thinker, just living by hope.

I talked with a man who, unlike that apple tree, is about forty years old—although he's one of the oldest fortyish men I have met in all my life. Seeing him on the street, I asked him how he was, a purely routine inquiry, and then I asked him how things were going, another routine inquiry. But he took my inquiries seriously, and for fifteen minutes he detailed for me how bad he felt and how terribly everything was going. I gathered after a while that he was deriving a kind of perverse pleasure from recounting all the failures he had had, like when you have a toothache and you get a certain pleasure out of grinding down on the tooth. He was getting pleasure out of the fact that everything had gone badly.

When I feebly tried to interject that maybe it

was not so bad, he instantly repudiated my optimism. He said, "I tell you, it's all bad." So I let him
have his say and finally he ran down. "There's the
whole sad story," he concluded. "I'm down at the
bottom. All I have left is hope."

"Why," I said, "congratulations!"

He looked at me suspiciously and asked,
"What are you congratulating me about?"

"Because you said you're down to hope," I told
him. "You've got all that mess of negativism
cleared away. All that old rotted stuff is cleared
away, and there remains the bright and shining
emergence of hope. Boy, you are really in luck. All

you have to do is to step up that hope and you will have the time of your life."

And of course he would, because hope is a marvelous force. Here is a saying from the Bible about hope, in 1 Corinthians: "And now abideth faith, hope, charity, these three; but the greatest of these is charity." Then what is the second greatest? It is hope and/or faith. The three greatest words in the English language—and one of them is hope.

You know the old saying that where there is life, there is hope. I suggest you turn it around: Where there is hope, there is life. You're never defeated, you're never beaten down, as long as you have hope.

*The future belongs to those
who believe in the beauty
of their dreams.*
ELEANOR ROOSEVELT

Keep this thought in mind. Keep it in mind always as difficulties and sorrows and sickness and trouble come upon you. Keep in mind always that, like the springtime, hope always comes back.

$\mathscr{H}$ope is a great thing. It even has a therapeutic value. Do you want to feel better? Take a big dose of hope. It will do wonders for you. I think it must have a salutary effect on the organs and glands of the body. I feel energized just from talking about it!

I read about a man, eighty-seven years of age,

who was killed by a truck hitting him. He'd been a very active man until the day he died. At the hospital where he was taken, they later performed an autopsy. And the surgeon said to the widow, "Madam, your husband must have been a very remarkable man, for I have examined his organs and he had enough wrong with him that he should have died thirty years ago. It's amazing. I can't understand how a man with all that was wrong with him on the inside lived as long as he did. How do you explain it?"

"Well," she said, "I can only tell you this: My husband always had an optimistic point of view. He never went to bed any night of his life that he didn't say, 'I'm going to feel better tomorrow.' And," she added, "he was always saying, 'I have hopes.'"

Isn't that wonderful? "I have hopes!" Yes, things are bad—but I have hopes. Yes, things are dark—but I have hopes. If you want to live to eighty-seven, this is a good way to do it.

*H*ope is a dynamic word that can change your life. Write this word in gigantic letters across the sky of your life, deeply embed it in your consciousness, condition your attitudes around hope until it becomes a very part of your being, and then your life will be good, very good, no matter how much pain or difficulty you may encounter.

Breathe the fresh air into your lungs and *hope* into your mind. Remember that you do not go into the world alone, but with God, who has walked with you ever since you were a child, and the Lord Jesus Christ is with you too. Begin tomorrow with hope. Unlock the mysterious door of the future with the golden key of hope in God.